Poems
that Stir
the Heart

Poems that Stir the Heart

COMPILED BY MARY SANFORD LAURENCE

A HART BOOK

A & W PUBLISHERS • NEW YORK

PUBLISHED BY
A & W PUBLISHERS, INC.
95 MADISON AVENUE
NEW YORK, NEW YORK 10016

LIBRARY OF CONGRESS CATALOG CARD NO. 79-65344

ISBN: 0-89479-057-9

PRINTED IN THE UNITED STATES OF AMERICA

Contents

CELEBRATION

CHILDREN

COMPASSION

COURAGE

FULFILLMENT

GRIEF

Foreword

Have you ever felt something so strongly that it seemed like ordinary words couldn't express your emotion? Perhaps you wanted to tell a friend how much you valued him, or maybe you wanted to give hope to someone who was caught in the clutches of the Giant Despair. Perhaps your heart was full with a sense of joy in nature, or with grief at the loss of a loved one.

In such moments, we often turn to poetry. Poetry satisfies our longing for beauty and for inspiration. Poetry cheers us when we're sad, or lonely. Poetry comforts us when we lose our loved ones, or feel nostalgia for the past. Poetry entertains us, moves us, strengthens us, gives voice to the thoughts that, as Wordsworth said, "do often lie too deep for tears." That's why, for thousand of years, poems have been written and read.

This collection of verses contains many of the favorite poems of the American people. Here are poems about brotherhood, desire, courage, and love. Here are poems of celebration, of inspiration, of thankfulness; poems to renew our faith in God and in human goodness; poems to help us have patience in times of trial, and poems to tell those closest to us how much they mean to us. This is not an anthology of academic poems for scholars, but a selection of verses that have touched and stirred the hearts of millions of ordinary human beings for many years. Here are poems by Alfred Tennyson and Edgar Guest, Christina Rossetti and Margaret E. Sangster, and many other poets. Some of the poets in this volume are well-known; some are not so well known. But all of them had the ability to express the deep emotions that come to everyone, to give words to the various moods, feelings, and thoughts that are a part of our human make-up. Here are poems to read and reread, whenever we are deeply moved.

AFFECTION

At Nightfall

I need so much the quiet of your love
    After the day's loud strife;
I need your calm all other things above
    After the stress of life.

I crave the haven that in your dear heart lies,
    After all toil is done;
I need the starshine of your heavenly eyes,
    After the day's great sun.

CHARLES HANSON TOWNE

Love's Philosophy

The fountains mingle with the river,
    And the rivers with the ocean;
The winds of heaven mix forever,
    With a sweet emotion;
Nothing in the world is single;
    All things by a law divine
In one another's being mingle:—
    Why not I with thine?

See! the mountains kiss high heaven,
    And the waves clasp one another;
No sister flower would be forgiven
    If it disdained its brother;
And the sunlight clasps the earth,
    And the moonbeams kiss the sea:—
What are all these kissings worth,
    If thou kiss not me?

PERCY BYSSHE SHELLEY

Death, Be Not Proud

Death, be not proud, though some have called thee
    Mighty and dreadful, for thou art not so;
    For those whom thou think'st thou dost overthrow
Die not, poor Death, nor yet canst thou kill me.
From rest and sleep, which but thy pictures be,
    Much pleasure; then from thee much more must flow,
    And soonest our best men with thee do go,
Rest of their bones, and soul's delivery.

Thou art slave to fate, chance, kings, and desperate men,
    And dost with poison, war, and sickness dwell;
    And poppy or charms can make us sleep as well
And better than thy stroke; why swell'st thou then?
    One short sleep past, we wake eternally,
    And death shall be no more; Death, thou shalt die.

JOHN DONNE

18

Requiescat

Strew on her roses, roses,
  And never a spray of yew:
In quiet she reposes;
  Ah, would that I did too!

Her mirth the world required;
  She bathed it in smiles of glee.
But her heart was tired, tired,
  And now they let her be.

Her life was turning, turning,
  In mazes of heat and sound.
But for peace her soul was yearning,
  And now peace laps her round.

Her cabined, ample spirit,
  It fluttered and failed for breath;
Tonight it doth inherit
  The vasty hall of death.

MATTHEW ARNOLD

The Stone

"And you will cut a stone for him,
To set above his head?
And will you cut a stone for him—
A stone for him?" she said.

Three days before, a splintered rock
Had struck her lover dead—
Had struck him in the quarry dead,
Where, careless of the warning call,
He loitered, while the shot was fired—
A lively stripling, brave and tall,
And sure of all his heart desired. . .
A flash, a shock,
A rumbing fall. . .
And, broken 'neath the broken rock,
A lifeless heap, with face of clay;
And still as any stone he lay,
With eyes that saw the end of all.

I went to break the news to her;
And I could hear my own heart beat
With dread of what my lips might say
But, some poor fool had sped before;
And flinging wide her father's door,

Had blurted out the news to her,
Had struck her lover dead for her,
Had struck the girl's heart dead in her,
Had struck life lifeless at a word,
And dropped it at her feet:
Then hurried on his witless way,
Scarce knowing she had heard.

And when I came, she stood alone,
A woman turned to stone:
And, though no word at all she said,
I knew that all was known.
Because her heart was dead,
She did not sigh nor moan,
His mother wept;
She could not weep.
Her lover slept:
She could not sleep.
Three days, three nights,
She did not stir:
Three days, three nights,
Were one to her,
Who never closed her eyes
From sunset to sunrise,
From dawn to evenfall:
Her tearless, staring eyes,
That seeing naught, saw all.

The fourth night when I came from work,
I found her at my door.
"And will you cut a stone for him?"
She said: and spoke no more:
But followed me, as I went in,
And sank upon a chair;
And curdled the warm blood in me,
Those eyes that cut me to the bone,
And pierced my marrow like cold steel.

And so I rose, and sought a stone;
And cut it, smooth and square:
And, as I worked, she sat and watched,
Beside me, in her chair.
Night after night, by candlelight,
I cut her lover's name:
Night after night, so still and white,
And like a ghost she came;
And sat beside me in her chair;
And watched with eyes aflame.
She eyed each stroke;
And hardly stirred:
She never spoke
A single word:
And not a sound or murmur broke
The quiet, save the mallet-stroke.
With still eyes ever on my hands,
With eyes that seemed to burn my hands,

22

My wincing, overwearied hands,
She watched, with bloodless lips apart,
And silent, indrawn breath:
And every stroke my chisel cut,
Death cut still deeper in her heart:
The two of us were chiseling,
Together, I and death.

And when at length the job was done,
And I had laid the mallet by,
As if, at last, her peace were won,
She breathed his name; and, with a sigh,
Passed slowly through the open door:
And never crossed my threshold more.

Next night I labored late, alone.
To cut her name upon the stone.

WILFRED WILSON GIBSON

Requiescat

Tread lightly, she is near
    Under the snow,
Speak gently, she can hear
    The daisies grow.

All her bright golden hair
    Tarnished with rust,
She that was young and fair
    Fallen to dust.

Lily-like, white as snow,
    She hardly knew
She was a woman, so
    Sweetly she grew.

Coffin-board, heavy stone,
    Lie on her breast;
I vex my heart alone,
    She is at rest.

Peace, peace; she cannoth hear
    Lyre or sonnet;
All my life's buried here.
    Heap earth upon it.

OSCAR WILDE

BROTHERHOOD

The Human Touch

'Tis the human touch in this world that counts,
    The touch of your hand and mine,
Which means far more to the fainting heart
    Than shelter and bread and wine;
For shelter is gone when the night is o'er,
    And bread lasts only a day,
But the touch of the hand and the sound of the voice
    Sing on in the soul alway.

SPENCER MICHAEL FREE

The House by the Side of the Road

There are hermit souls that live withdrawn
    In the peace of their self-content;
There are souls, like stars, that dwell apart,
    In a fellowless firmament;
There are pioneer souls that blaze their paths
    Where highways never ran;
But let me live by the side of the road
    And be a friend to man.

Let me live in a house by the side of the road,
    Where the race of men go by—
The men who are good and the men who are bad,
    As good and as bad as I.
I would not sit in the scorner's seat,
    Or hurl the cynic's ban;
Let me live in a house by the side of the road
    And be a friend to man.

I see from my house by the side of the road,
    By the side of the highway of life,
The men who press with the ardor of hope,
    The men who are faint with the strife.
But I turn not away from their smiles
        nor their tears—
    Both parts of an infinite plan;
Let me live in my house by the side of the road
    And be a friend to man.

Let me live in my house by the side of the road
    Where the race of men go by—
They are good, they are bad, they are weak,
        they are strong,
    Wise, foolish—so am I.
Then why should I sit in the scorner's seat
    Or hurl the cynic's bar?—
Let me live in my house by the side of the road
    And be a friend to man.

SAM WALTER FOSS

Welcome Over the Door of an Old Inn

Hail, Guest! We ask not what thou art;
If Friend, we greet thee, hand and heart;
If Stranger, such no longer be;
If Foe, our love shall conquer thee.

ARTHUR GUITERMAN

What Was His Creed?

What was his creed?
I do not know his creed, I only know
That here below, he walked the common road
And lifted many a load, lightened the task,
Brightened the day for others toiling on a weary way:
This, his only meed; I do not know his creed.

His creed? I care not what his creed;
Enough that never yielded he to greed,
But served a brother in his daily need;
Plucked many a thorn and planted many a flower;
Glorified the service of each hour;
Had faith in God, himself, and fellow-men;—
Perchance he never thought in terms of creed,
I only know he lived a life, in deed!

H.N. FIFER

The Voice of God

I sought to hear the voice of God,
  And climbed the topmost steeple.
But God declared: "Go down again,
  I dwell among the people."

LOUIS I. NEWMAN

Plea for Tolerance

If we but knew what forces helped to mold
    The lives of others from their earliest years—
    Knew something of their background, joys and
        tears,
And whether or not their youth was drear and cold,
Or if some dark belief had taken hold
    And kept them shackled, torn with doubts and
        fears
    So long it crushed the force that perseveres
And made their hearts grow prematurely old,—

Then we might judge with wiser, kindlier sight,
    And learn to put aside our pride and scorn . . .
Perhaps no one can ever quite undo
    His faults or wholly banish some past blight—
The tolerant mind is purified, reborn,
    And lifted upward to a saner view.

MARGARET E. BRUNER

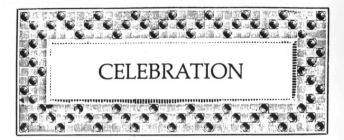

Ring Out, Wild Bells

Ring out, wild bells, to the wild sky,
　　The flying cloud, the frosty light:
　　The year is dying in the night;
Ring out, wild bells, and let him die.

Ring out the old, ring in the new,
　　Ring, happy bells, across the snow:
　　The year is going, let him go;
Ring out the false, ring in the true.

ALFRED, LORD TENNYSON

Trees

I think that I shall never see
A poem as lovely as a tree.

A tree whose hungry mouth is prest
Against the earth's sweet flowing breast;

A tree that looks at God all day,
And lifts her leafy arms to pray;

A tree that may in Summer wear
A nest of robins in her hair;

Upon whose bosom snow has lain;
Who intimately lives with rain.

Poems are made by fools like me,
But only God can make a tree.

JOYCE KILMER

The Daffodils

I wandered lonely as a cloud
    That floats on high o'er vales and hills,
When all at once I saw a crowd,
    A host, of golden daffodils,
Beside the lake, beneath the trees,
Fluttering and dancing in the breeze.

Continuous as the stars that shine
    And twinkle on the milky way,
They stretched in never-ending line
    Along the margin of a bay:
Ten thousand saw I at a glance
Tossing their heads in sprightly dance.

The waves beside them danced, but they
    Out-did the sparkling waves in glee:
A Poet could not but be gay
    In such a jocund company!
I gazed—and gazed—but little thought
What wealth the show to me had brought:

For oft, when on my couch I lie
    In vacant or in pensive mood,
They flash upon that inward eye
    Which is the bliss of solitude;
And then my heart with pleasure fills,
And dances with the daffodils.

WILLIAM WORDSWORTH

Holidays

The holiest of all holidays are those
Kept by ourselves in silence and apart;
The secret anniversaries of the heart.

HENRY WADSWORTH LONGFELLOW

CHILDREN

On Going Home for Christmas

He little knew the sorrow that was in his vacant
    chair;
He never guessed they'd miss him, or he'd surely have
    been there;
He couldn't see his mother or the lump that filled her
    throat,
Or the tears that started falling as she read his hasty
    note;
And he couldn't see his father, sitting sorrowful and
    dumb,
Or he never would have written that he thought he
    couldn't come.

He little knew the gladness that his presence would
      have made,
And the joy it would have given, or he never would
      have stayed.
He didn't know how hungry had the little mother
      grown
Once again to see her baby and to claim him for her
      own.
He didn't guess the meaning of his visit Christmas
      Day
Or he never would have written that he couldn't get
      away.

He couldn't see the fading of the cheeks that once
      were pink,
And the silver in the tresses; and he didn't stop to
      think
How the years are passing swiftly, and next Christmas
      it might be
There would be no home to visit and no mother dear
      to see.
He didn't think about it—I'll not say he didn't care.
He was heedless and forgetful or he'd surely have
      been there.

Are you going home for Christmas? Have you written
     you'll be there?
Going home to kiss the mother and to show her that
     you care?
Going home to greet the father in a way to make him
     glad?
If you're not I hope there'll never come a time you'll
     wish you had.
Just sit down and write a letter—it will make their
     heartstrings hum
With a tune of perfect gladness—if you'll tell them
     that you'll come.

EDGAR GUEST

Children

Your children are not your children.

They are the sons and daughters of Life's longing for
itself.

They come through you but not from you,

And though they are with you yet they belong not to
you.

You may give them your love but not your thoughts,

For they have their own thoughts.

You may house their bodies but not their souls,

For their souls dwell in the house of tomorrow, which
you cannot visit, not even in your dreams.

You may strive to be like them, but seek not to make
them like you.

For life goes not backward nor tarries with yesterday.

KAHLIL GIBRAN

To a New Daughter-in-Law

Forgive me if I speak possessively of him
    Who now is yours, yet still is mine;
Call it the silver cord disparagingly
    And weave new colors in an old design,
Yet know the warp was started long ago
    By faltering steps, by syllable and sound,
By all the years in which I watched him grow. . . .
    By all the seasons' turnings are we bound.

But now, I loose the cord, untie the knot,
    Unravel years so he is yours alone
And if there is a message I forgot
      Or something that could help you had you
          known,
        I shall be waiting, hoping you will see
        That him you love, is also *loved by me.*

AUTHOR UNKNOWN

To My Son

Do you know that your soul is of my soul such part,
That you seem to be fibre and cord of my heart?
None other can pain me as you, dear, can do,
None other can please me or praise me as you.

Remember the world will be quick with its blame
If shadow or stain ever darken your name,
"Like mother like son" is a saying so true,
The world will judge largely of "Mother" by you.

Be yours then the task, if task it shall be
To force the proud world to do homage to me,
Be sure it will say when its verdict you've won,
"She reaped as she sowed, Lo! this is her son."

MARGARET JOHNSTON GRIFFIN

Patty-Poem

She never puts her toys away;
Just leaves them scattered where they lay—
I try to scold her, and I say
    "You make me mad!"

But when to bed she has to chase,
The toys she left about the place
Remind me of her shining face,
    And make me glad.

When she grows up and gathers poise
I'll miss her harum-scarum noise,
And look in vain for scattered toys—
    And I'll be sad.

NICK KENNY

If I Can Stop One Heart From Breaking

If I can stop one heart from breaking,
  I shall not live in vain;
If I can ease one life the aching,
  Or cool one pain,
Or help one lonely person
  Into happiness again
I shall not live in vain.

EMILY DICKINSON

Prayer for Shut-ins

Because, dear Lord, their way is rough and steep,
And some are sore perplexed, and some do weep,
We come to ask that Thou wilt show the way
And give Thy rod and staff to be their stay.

Especially, dear Lord, for these we ask,
Who have not strength to meet their task;
And for all weary on the road
Please give fresh courage, ease their load.

RUTH WINANT WHEELER

Life Lesson

There! little girl; don't cry!
   They have broken your doll, I know;
      And your tea-set blue,
      And your play-house, too,
   Are things of the long ago;
      But childish troubles will soon pass by
        There! little girl; don't cry!

There! little girl; don't cry!
   They have broken your slate, I know;
      And the glad, wild ways
      Of your school-girl days
   Are things of the long ago;
      But life and love will soon come by.
        There! little girl; don't cry!

There! little girl; don't cry!
   They have broken your heart, I know;
      And the rainbow gleams
      Of your youthful dreams
   Are things of the long ago;
      But heaven holds all for which you sigh.
        There! little girl; don't cry!

JAMES WHITCOMB RILEY

Song of the Shirt

With fingers weary and worn,
    With eyelids heavy and red,
A woman sat in unwomanly rags,
    Plying her needle and thread—
Stitch! stitch! stitch!
    In poverty, hunger, and dirt,
And still with a voice of dolorous pitch
    She sang the "Song of the Shirt!"

"Work—work—work
    Till the brain begins to swim;
Work—work—work
    Till the eyes are heavy and dim!
Seam, and gusset, and band,
    Band, and gusset, and seam,
Till over the buttons I fall asleep,
    And sew them on in a dream!

"O men, with sisters dear!
    O men, with mothers and wives!
It is not linen you're wearing out,
    But human creatures' lives!
Stitch—stitch—stitch!
    In poverty, hunger, and dirt —
Sewing at once, with a double thread,
    A shroud as well as a shirt!

"But why do I talk of Death—
    That phantom of grisly bone?
I hardly fear his terrible shape,
    It seems so like my own,—
It seems so like my own
    Because of the fasts I keep;
O God! that bread should be so dear,
    And flesh and blood so cheap!

"Work! work! work!
    My labor never flags;
And what are its wages? A bed of straw,
    A crust of bread—and rags.
That shattered roof—and this naked floor—
    A table—a broken chair—
And a wall so bland, my shadow I thank
    For sometimes falling there!

"Work—work—work!
    From weary chime to chime!
Work—work—work!
    As prisoners work for crime!
Band, and gusset, and seam,
    Seam, and gusset, and band —
Till the heart is sick and the brain benumbed,
    As well as the weary hand.

"Work—work—work!
    In the dull December light!
And work—work—work!
    When the weather is warm and bright!
While underneath the eaves
    The brooding swallows cling,
As if to show me their sunny backs,
    And twit me with the spring.

"Oh, but for one short hour—
    A respite, however brief!
No blessed leisure for love or hope,
    But only time for grief!
A little weeping would ease my heart;
    But in their briny bed
My tears must stop, for every drop
    Hinders needle and thread!"

With fingers weary and worn,
    With eyelids heavy and red,
A woman sat in unwomanly rags,
    Plying her needle and thread—
Stitch! stitch! stitch!
    In poverty, hunger, and dirt;
And still with a voice of dolorous pitch—
Would that its tone could reach the rich!—
    She sang this "Song of the Shirt."

THOMAS HOOD

49

COURAGE

It Can be Done

The man who misses all the fun
Is he who says, "It can't be done."
In solemn pride he stands aloof
And greets each venture with reproof.
Had he the power he'd efface
The history of the human race;
We'd have no radio or motor cars,
No streets lit by electric stars;
No telegraph nor telephone,
We'd linger in the age of stone.
The world would sleep if things were run
By men who say, "It can't be done."

AUTHOR UNKNOWN

Invictus

Out of the night that covers me,
    Black as the Pit from pole to pole,
I thank whatever gods may be
    For my unconquerable soul.

In the fell clutch of circumstance
    I have not winced nor cried aloud.
Under the bludgeonings of chance
    My head is bloody, but unbowed.

Beyond this place of wrath and tears
    Looms but the horror of the shade,
And yet the menace of the years
    Finds, and shall find me, unafraid.

It matters not how strait the gate,
    How charged with punishments the scroll,
I am the master of my fate:
    I am the captain of my soul.

WILLIAM ERNEST HENLEY

Defeat

No one is beat till he quits,
    No one is through till he stops,
No matter how hard Failure hits,
    No matter how often he drops,
A fellow's not down till he lies
In the dust and refuses to rise.

Fate can slam him and bang him around,
    And batter his frame till he's sore,
But she never can say that he's downed
    While he bobs up serenely for more.
A fellow's not dead till he dies,
Nor beat till no longer he tries.

EDGAR GUEST

You Mustn't Quit

When things go wrong, as they sometimes will,
When the road you're trudging seems all uphill,
When the funds are low and the debts are high
And you want to smile, but you have to sigh,
When care is pressing you down a bit,
Rest! if you must—but never quit.

Life is queer, with its twists and turns,
As every one of us sometimes learns,
And many a failure turns about
When he might have won if he'd stuck it out;
Stick to your task, though the pace seems slow—
You may succeed with one more blow.

Success is failure turned inside out—
The silver tint of the clouds of doubt—
And you never can tell how close you are,
It may be near when it seems afar;
So stick to the fight when you're hardest hit—
It's when things seem worst that YOU MUSTN'T QUIT.

AUTHOR UNKNOWN

If—

If you can keep your head when all about you
    Are losing theirs and blaming it on you;
If you can trust yourself when all men doubt you,
    But make allowance for their doubting too;
If you can wait and not be tired by waiting,
    Or, being lied about, don't deal in lies,
Or, being hated, don't give way to hating,
    And yet don't look too good, nor talk too wise;

If you can dream—and not make dreams your
      master;
    If you can think—and not make thoughts your
      aim;
If you can meet with triumph and disaster
    And treat those two impostors just the same;
If you can bear to hear the truth you've spoken
    Twisted by knaves to make a trap for fools,
Or watch the things you gave your life to broken,
    And stoop and build 'em up with worn out tools;

If you can make one heap of all your winnings
    And risk it on one turn of pitch-and-toss,
And lose, and start again at your beginnings
    And never breathe a word about your loss;
If you can force your heart and nerve and sinew
    To serve your turn long after they are gone,
And so hold on when there is nothing in you
    Except the Will which says to them: "Hold on!"

If you can talk with crowds and keep your virtue,
    Or walk with kings—nor lose the common touch;
If neither foes nor loving friends can hurt you;
    If all men count with you, but none too much;
If you can fill the unforgiving minute
    With sixty seconds' worth of distance run—
Yours is the Earth and everything that's in it,
    And—which is more—you'll be a Man, my son!

RUDYARD KIPLING

DESIRE

The Indian Serenade

I arise from dreams of thee
In the first sweet sleep of night,
When the winds are breathing low,
And the stars are shining bright
I arise from dreams of thee,
And a spirit in my feet
Hath led me—who knows how?
To thy chamber window, Sweet!

The wandering airs they faint
On the dark, the silent stream—
The champak odors fail
Like sweet thoughts in a dream;
The nightingale's complaint,
It dies upon her heart;
As I must on thine,
Oh, beloved as thou art!

O lift me from the grass!
I die! I faint! I fail!
Let thy love in kisses rain
On my lips and eyelids pale.
My cheek is cold and white, alas!
My heart beats loud and fast;—
Oh! press it to thine own again,
Where it will break at last.

PERCY BYSSHE SHELLEY

Faithful to Thee, in My Fashion

Last night, ah, yesternight, betwixt her lips and mine
　　There fell thy shadow, Cynara! thy breath was
　　　　shed
Upon my soul between the kisses and the wine;
　　　And I was desolate and sick of an old passion,
　　Yea, I was desolate and bowed my head:
　　　I have been faithful to thee, Cynara! in my
　　　　fashion.

All night upon mine heart I felt her warm heart beat,
　　Night-long within mine arms in love and sleep she
　　　　lay;
Surely the kisses of her bought red mouth were sweet;
　　　But I was desolate and sick of an old passion,
　　When I awoke and found the dawn was gray:
　　　I have been faithful to thee, Cynara! in my
　　　　fashion.

I have forgot much, Cynara! gone with the wind,
  Flung roses, roses riotously with the throng,
Dancing, to put thy pale, lost lilies out of mind;
    But I was desolate and sick of an old passion,
  Yea, all the time, because the dance was long:
    I have been faithful to thee, Cynara! in my
      fashion.

I cried for madder music and for stronger wine,
  But when the feast is finished and the lamps
      expire,
Then falls thy shadow, Cynara! the night is thine;
    And I am desolate and sick of an old passion,
  Yea, hungry for the lips of my desire:
    I have been faithful to thee, Cynara! in my
      fashion.

ERNEST DOWSON

I Love You

I love your lips when they're wet with wine
    And red with a wild desire;
I love your eyes when the lovelight lies
    Lit with a passionate fire.
I love your arms when the strands enmesh
    Your kisses against my face.

Not for me the cold, calm kiss
    Of a virgin's bloodless love;
Not for me the saint's white bliss,
    Nor the heart of a spotless dove.
But give me the love that so freely gives
    And laughs at the whole world's blame,
With your body so young and warm in my arms,
    It set my poor heart aflame.

So kiss me sweet with your warm wet mouth,
    Still fragrant with ruby wine,
And say with a fervor born of the South
    That you body and soul are mine.
Clasp me close in your warm young arms,
    While the pale stars shine above,
And we'll live our whole young lives away
    In the joys of a living love.

ELLA WHEELER WILCOX

FACING DEATH

Requiem

Under the wide and starry sky,
Dig the grave and let me lie.
Glad did I live and gladly die,
    And I laid me down with a will.

This be the verse you grave for me:
Here he lies where he longed to be;
Home is the sailor, home from sea,
    And the hunter home from the hill.

ROBERT LOUIS STEVENSON

Good-Bye

Good-bye, proud world! I'm going home:
Thou art not my friend, and I'm not thine.
Long through thy weary crowds I roam;
A river-ark on the ocean brine,
Long I've been tossed like the driven foam;
But now, proud world! I'm going home.

Good-bye to Flattery's fawning face;
To Grandeur with his wise grimace;
To upstart Wealth's averted eye;
To supple Office, low and high;
To crowded halls, to court and street;
To frozen hearts and hasting feet;
To those who go, and those who come;
Good-bye, proud world! I'm going home.

I am going to my own hearth-stone,
Bosomed in yon green hills alone—
A secret nook in a pleasant land,
Whose groves the frolic fairies planned;
Where arches green, the livelong day,
Echo the blackbird's roundelay,
And vulgar feet have never trod
A spot that is sacred to thought and God.

O, when I am safe in my sylvan home,
I tread on the pride of Greece and Rome;
And when I am stretched beneath the pines,
Where the evening star so holy shines,
I laugh at the lore and the pride of man,
At the sophist schools and the learned clan;
For what are they all, in their high conceit,
When man in the bush with God may meet?

RALPH WALDO EMERSON

Crossing the Bar

Sunset and evening star,
    And one clear call for me!
And may there be no moaning of the bar,
    When I put out to sea.

But such a tide as moving seems asleep,
    Too full for sound and foam,
When that which drew from out the boundless deep
    Turns again home.

Twilight and evening bell,
    And after that the dark!
And may there be no sadness of farewell,
    When I embark;

For tho' from out our bourne of Time and Place
    The flood may bear me far,
I hope to see my Pilot face to face
    When I have crost the bar.

ALFRED, LORD TENNYSON

So Live

So live that when thy summons comes to join
The innumerable caravan, which moves
To that mysterious realm, where each shall take
His chamber in the silent halls of death,
Thou go not like the quarry slave at night,
Scourged to his dungeon, but, sustained and soothed
By an unfaltering trust, approach thy grave
Like one who wraps the drapery of his couch
About him, and lies down to pleasant dreams.

(FROM "THANATOPSIS") WILLIAM CULLEN BRYANT

When I Am Dead, My Dearest

When I am dead, my dearest,
   Sing no sad songs for me;
Plant thou no roses at my head,
   Nor shady cypress-tree:
Be the green grass above me
   With showers and dewdrops wet;
And if thou wilt, remember,
   And if thou wilt, forget.

I shall not see the shadows,
   I shall not feel the rain;
I shall not hear the nightingale
   Sing on, as if in pain:
And dreaming through the twilight
   That doth not rise nor set,
Haply I may remember,
   And haply may forget.

CHRISTINA ROSSETTI

Take the World as It Is

Take the world as it is!—with its smiles and its
　　sorrow,
　　Its love and its friendship—its falsehood and
　　　　truth—
Its schemes that depend on the breath of tomorrow!
　　Its hopes which pass by like the dreams of our
　　　　youth—
Yet, oh! whilst the light of affection may shine,
　　The heart in itself hath a fountain of bliss!
In the *worst* there's some spark of a nature divine,
　　And the wisest and best *take the world as it is.*

CHARLES SWAIN

On His Blindness

When I consider how my light is spent
    Ere half my days in this dark world and wide,
    And that one talent which is death to hide
Lodged with me useless, though my soul more bent
To serve therewith my Maker, and present
    My true account, lest he returning chide,
    "Doth God exact day-labor, light denied?"
I fondly ask. But Patience, to prevent
That murmur, soon replies, "God doth not need
    Either man's work or his own gifts. Who best
    Bear his mild yoke, they serve him best. His state
Is kingly: thousands at his bidding speed,
    And post o'er land and ocean without rest;
    They also serve who only stand and wait."

JOHN MILTON

One Year to Live

If I had but one year to live;
One year to help; one year to give;
One year to love; one year to bless;
One year of better things to stress;
One year to sing; one year to smile;
To brighten earth a little while;
I think that I would spend each day,
In just the very self-same way
That I do now. For from afar
The call may come to cross the bar
At any time, and I must be
Prepared to meet eternity.
So if I have a year to live,
Or just a day in which to give
A pleasant smile, a helping hand,
A mind that tries to understand
A fellow-creature when in need,
'Tis one with me,—I take no heed;
But try to live each day He sends
To serve my gracious Master's ends.

MARY DAVIS REED

High Resolve

I'll hold my candle high, and then
Perhaps I'll see the hearts of men
Above the sordidness of life,
Beyond misunderstandings, strife.
Though many deeds that others do
Seem foolish, rash and sinful too,
Just who am I to criticize
What I perceive with my dull eyes?
I'll hold my candle high, and then,
Perhaps I'll see the hearts of men.

AUTHOR UNKNOWN

A Bag of Tools

Isn't it strange
    That princes and kings,
And clowns that caper
    In sawdust rings,
And common people
    Like you and me
    Are builders for eternity?

Each is given a bag of tools,
    A shapeless mass,
A book of rules;
    And each must make—
Ere life is flown—
    A stumbling block
Or a steppingstone.

R.L. SHARPE

The Junk Box

My father often used to say:
"My boy don't throw a thing away:
You'll find a use for it some day."

So in a box he stored up things,
Bent nails, old washers, pipes and rings,
And bolts and nuts and rusty springs.

Despite each blemish and each flaw,
Some use for everything he saw;
With things material, this was law.

And often when he'd work to do,
He searched the junk box through and through
And found old stuff as good as new.

And I have often thought since then,
That father did the same with men;
He knew he'd need their help again.

It seems to me he understood
That men, as well as iron and wood,
May broken be and still be good.

Despite the vices he'd display
He never threw a man away,
But kept him for another day.

A human junk box is this earth
And into it we're tossed at birth,
To wait the day we'll be of worth.

Though bent and twisted, weak of will,
And full of flaws and lacking skill,
Some service each can render still.

EDGAR GUEST

Worthwhile

It is easy enough to be pleasant,
   When life flows by like a song,
But the man worthwhile is one who will smile,
   When everything goes dead wrong.
For the test of the heart is trouble,
   And it always comes with the years,
And the smile that is worth the praises of earth
   Is the smile that shines through tears.

It is easy enough to be prudent,
   When nothing tempts you to stray,
When without or within no voice of sin
   Is luring your soul away;
But it's only a negative virtue
   Until it is tried by fire,
And the life that is worth the honor on earth
   Is the one that resists desire.

By the cynic, the sad, the fallen,
    Who had no strength for the strife,
The world's highway is cumbered today;
    They make up the sum of life.
But the virtue that conquers passion,
    And the sorrow that hides in a smile,
It is these that are worth the homage on earth
    For we find them but once in a while.

ELLA WHEELER WILCOX

Then Laugh

Build for yourself a strong box,
    Fashion each part with care;
When it's strong as your hand can make it,
    Put all your troubles there;
Hide there all thought of your failures,
    And each bitter cup that you quaff;
Lock all your heartaches within it,
    Then sit on the lid and laugh.

Tell no one else its contents,
    Never its secrets share;
When you've dropped in your care and worry
    Keep them forever there;
Hide them from sight so completely
    That the world will never dream half;
Fasten the strong box securely—
    Then sit on the lid and laugh.

BERTHA ADAMS BACKUS

FAITH

I Never Saw a Moor

I never saw a moor,
I never saw the sea;
Yet know I how the heather looks,
And what a wave must be.

I never spoke with God,
Nor visited in Heaven;
Yet certain am I of the spot
As if the chart were given.

EMILY DICKINSON

What Thomas an Buile Said in a Pub

I saw God. Do you doubt it?
    Do you dare to doubt it?
I saw the Almighty Man. His hand
Was resting on a mountain, and
He looked upon the World and all about it:
I saw Him plainer than you see me now,
    You mustn't doubt it.

He was not satisfied;
    His look was all dissatisfied.
His beard swung on a wind far out of sight
Behind the world's curve, and there was light
Most fearful from His forehead, and He sighed,
"That star went always wrong, and from the start
    I was dissatisfied."

He lifted up His hand—
    I say He heaved a dreadful hand
Over the spinning Earth. Then I said, "Stay,
You must not strike it, God; I'm in the way;
And I will never move from where I stand."
He said, "Dear child, I feared that you were dead,"
    And stayed His hand.

JAMES STEPHENS

A Prayer for Faith

God, give me back the simple faith
    that I so long have clung to,
  My simple faith in peace and hope,
    in loveliness and light—
Because without this faith of mine,
    the rhythms I have sung to
  Become as empty as the sky upon a starless night.

God, let me feel that right is right,
    that reason dwells with reason,
  And let me feel that something grows
    whenever there is rain—
And let me sense that splendid truth
    that season follows season,
  And let me dare to dream
    that there is tenderness in pain.

God, give me back my simple faith
    because my soul is straying
  Away from all the little creeds
    that I so long have known;
Oh, answer me while still I have
    at least the strength for praying,
  For if the prayer dies from my heart
    I will be quite alone.

MARGARET E. SANGSTER

Faith

I will not doubt, though all my ships at sea
    Come drifting home with broken masts and sails;
    I shall believe the Hand which never fails,
From seeming evil worketh good to me;
      And, though I weep because those sails are
        battered,
      Still will I cry, while my best hopes lie shattered,
        "I trust in Thee."

I will not doubt, though all my prayers return
    Unanswered from the still, white realm above;
    I shall believe it is an all-wise Love
Which has refused those things for which I yearn;
      And though, at times, I cannot keep from
        grieving,
      Yet the pure ardor of my fixed believing
        Undimmed shall burn.

I will not doubt, though sorrows fall like rain,
    And troubles swarm like bees about a hive;
    I shall believe the heights for which I strive,
Are only reached by anguish and by pain;
    And, though I groan and tremble with my crosses,
    I yet shall see, through my severest losses,
        The greater gain.

I will not doubt; well anchored in the faith,
    Like some stanch ship, my soul braves every gale,
    So strong its courage that it will not fail
To breast the mighty, unknown sea of death.
    Oh, may I cry when body parts with spirit,
    "I do not doubt," so listening worlds may hear it
        With my last breath.

ELLA WHEELER WILCOX

Only a Dad

Only a dad with a tired face,
Coming home from the daily race,
Bringing little of gold or fame
To show how well he has played the game;
But glad in his heart that his own rejoice
To see him come and to hear his voice.

Only a dad with a brood of four,
One of ten million men or more
Plodding along in the daily strife,
Bearing the whips and the scorns of life,
With never a whimper of pain or hate,
For the sake of those who at home await.

Only a dad, neither rich nor proud,
Merely one of the surging crowd,
Toiling, striving from day to day,
Facing whatever may come his way,
Silent whenever the harsh condemn,
And bearing it all for the love of them.

Only a dad but he gives his all,
To smooth the way for his children small,
Doing with courage stern and grim
The deeds that his father did for him.
This is the line that for him I pen:
Only a dad, but the best of men.

EDGAR GUEST

Father

Used to wonder just why father
    Never had much time for play,
Used to wonder why he'd rather
    Work each minute of the day.
Used to wonder why he never
    Loafed along the road an' shirked;
Can't recall a time whenever
    Father played while others worked.

Father didn't dress in fashion,
    Sort of hated clothing new;
Style with him was not a passion;
    He had other things in view.
Boys are blind to much that's going
    On about 'em day by day,
And I had no way of knowing
    What became of father's pay.

All I knew was when I needed
    Shoes I got 'em on the spot;
Everything for which I pleaded,
    Somehow, father always got.

Wondered, season after season,
    Why he never took a rest,
And that *I* might be the reason
    Then I never even guessed.

Father set a store on knowledge;
    If he'd lived to have his way
He'd have sent me off to college
    And the bills been glad to pay.
That, I know, was his ambition:
    Now and then he used to say
He'd have done his earthly mission
    On my graduation day.

Saw his cheeks were getting paler,
    Didn't understand just why;
Saw his body growing frailer,
    Then at last I saw him die.
Rest had come! His tasks were ended
    Calm was written on his brow;
Father's life was big and splendid,
    And I understand it now.

EDGAR GUEST

FRIENDSHIP

Love

I love you,
Not only for what you are,
But for what I am
When I am with you.

I love you,
Not only for what
You have made of yourself,
But for what
You are making of me.

I love you
For the part of me
That you bring out;
I love you
For putting your hand
Into my heaped-up heart
And passing over
All the foolish, weak things
That you can't help
Dimly seeing there,
And for drawing out
Into the light
All the beautiful belongings
That no one else had looked
Quite far enough to find.

I love you because you
Are helping me to make
Of the lumber of my life
Not a tavern
But a temple;
Out of the works
Of my every day
Not a reproach
But a song.

I love you
Because you have done
More than any creed
Could have done
To make me good,
And more than any fate
Could have done
To make me happy.

You have done it
Without a touch,
Without a word,
Without a sign.
You have done it
By being yourself.
Perhaps that is what
Being a friend means,
After all.

ROY CROFT

Accept My Full Heart's Thanks

Your words came just when needed.
Like a breeze,
Blowing and bringing from the wide salt sea
Some cooling spray, to meadow scorched with heat
And choked with dust and clouds of sifted sand
That hateful whirlwinds, envious of its bloom,
Had tossed upon it. But the cool sea breeze
Came laden with the odors of the sea
And damp with spray, that laid the dust and sand
And brought new life and strength to blade and
     bloom
So words of thine came over miles to me,
Fresh from the mighty sea, a true friend's heart,
And brought me hope, and strength, and swept away
The dusty webs that human spiders spun
Across my path. Friend—and the word means
     much—
So few there are who reach like thee, a hand
Up over all the barking curs of spite
And give the clasp, when most its need is felt,
Friend, newly found, accept my full heart's thanks.

ELLA WHEELER WILCOX

Confide in a Friend

When you're tired and worn at the close of day
And things just don't seem to be going your way,
When even your patience has come to an end,
Try taking time out and confide in a friend.

Perhaps he too may have walked the same road
With a much troubled heart and burdensome load,
To find peace and comfort somewhere near the end,
When he stopped long enough to confide in a friend.

For then are most welcome a few words of cheer,
For someone who willingly lends you an ear.
No troubles exist that time cannot mend,
But to get quick relief, just confide in a friend.

AUTHOR UNKNOWN

Friendship

And let your best be for your friend.
If he must know the ebb of your tide, let him know
      its flood also.
For what is your friend that you should seek him with
      hours to kill?
Seek him always with hours to live.
For it is his to fill your need, but not your emptiness.
And in the sweetness of friendship let there be
      laughter, and sharing of pleasures.
For in the dew of little things the heart finds its
      morning and is refreshed.

Your friend is your needs answered.
He is your field which you sow with love and reap
      with thanksgiving.
And he is your board and your fireside.
For you come to him with your hunger, and you seek
      him for peace.

KAHLIL GIBRAN

The Arrow and the Song

I shot an arrow into the air,
It fell to earth, I knew not where;
For, so swiftly it flew, the sight
Could not follow it in its flight.

I breathed a song into the air,
It fell to earth, I knew not where;
For who has sight so keen and strong,
That it can follow the flight of song?

Long, long afterward, in an oak
I found the arrow, still unbroke;
And the song, from beginning to end,
I found again in the heart of a friend.

HENRY WADSWORTH LONGFELLOW

New Friends and Old Friends

Make new friends, but keep the old;
Those are silver, these are gold.
New-made friendships, like new wine,
Age will mellow and refine.
Friendships that have stood the test—
Time and change—are surely best;
Brow may wrinkle, hair grow gray;
Friendship never knows decay.
For 'mid old friends, tried and true,
Once more we our youth renew.
But old friends, alas! may die;
New friends must their place supply.
Cherish friendship in your breast—
New is good, but old is best;
Make new friends, but keep the old;
Those are silver, these are gold.

JOSEPH PARRY

To My Friend

I have never been rich before,
　　But you have poured
Into my heart's high door
　　A golden hoard.

My wealth is the vision shared,
　　The sympathy,
The feast of the soul prepared
　　By you for me.

Together we wander through
　　The wooded ways.
Old beauties are green and new
　　Seen through your gaze.

I look for no greater prize
　　Than your soft voice.
The steadiness of your eyes
　　Is my heart's choice.

I have never been rich before,
　　But I divine
Your step on my sunlit floor
　　And wealth is mine!

ANNE CAMPBELL

God Bless You

I seek in prayerful words, dear friend,
　　My heart's true wish to send you,
That you may know that, far or near,
　　My loving thoughts attend you.

I cannot find a truer word,
　　Nor better to address you;
Nor song, nor poem have I heard
　　Is sweeter than God bless you!

God bless you! So I've wished you all
　　Of brightness life possesses;
For can there any joy at all
　　Be yours unless God blesses?

God bless you! So I breathe a charm
　　Lest grief's dark night oppress you,
For how can sorrow bring you harm
　　If 'tis God's way to bless you?

And so, "through all thy days
　　May shadows touch thee never—"
But this alone—God bless thee—
　　Then art thou safe forever.

AUTHOR UNKNOWN

There Is Always
a Place for You

There is always a place for you at my table,
    You never need to be invited.
I'll share every crust as long as I'm able,
    And know you will be delighted.
There is always a place for you by my fire,
    And though it may burn to embers,
If warmth and good cheer are your desire
    The friend of your heart remembers!
There is always a place for you by my side,
    And should the years tear us apart,
I will face lonely moments more satisfied
    With a place for you in my heart!

ANNE CAMPBELL

Today

I have spread wet linen
On lavender bushes,
I have swept rose petals
From a garden walk.
I have labeled jars of raspberry jam,
I have baked a sunshine cake;
I have embroidered a yellow duck
On a small blue frock.
I have polished andirons,
Dusted the highboy,
Cut sweets peas for a black bowl,
Wound the tall clock,
Pleated a lace ruffle . . .
To-day
I have lived a poem.

ETHEL ROMIG FULLER

The Day Is Done

The day is done, and the darkness
    Falls from the wings of Night,
As a feather is wafted downward
    From an eagle in his flight.

I see the lights of the village
    Gleam through the rain and the mist,
And a feeling of sadness comes o'er me
    That my soul cannot resist:

A feeling of sadness and longing,
    That is not akin to pain,
And resembles sorrow only
    As the mist resembles the rain.

Come, read to me some poem,
    Some simple and heartfelt lay,
That shall soothe this restless feeling,
    And banish the thoughts of day.

Not from the grand old masters,
    Not from the bards sublime,
Whose distant footsteps echo
    Through the corridors of Time.

For, like strains of martial music,
    Their mighty thoughts suggest
Life's endless toil and endeavor;
    And tonight I long for rest.

Read from some humbler poet,
    Whose songs gushed from his heart,
As showers from the clouds of summer,
    Or tears from the eyelids start;

Who, through long days of labor,
    And nights devoid of ease,
Still heard in his soul the music
    Of wonderful melodies.

Such songs have power to quiet
    The restless pulse of care,
And come like the benediction
    That follows after prayer.

Then read from the treasured volume
    The poem of thy choice,
And lend to the rhyme of the poet
    The beauty of thy voice.

And the night shall be filled with music,
    And the cares, that infest the day,
Shall fold their tents, like the Arabs,
    And as silently steal away.

HENRY WADSWORTH LONGFELLOW

Thanks Be to God

I do not thank Thee, Lord,
That I have bread to eat while others starve;
Nor yet for work to do
While empty hands solicit Heaven;
Nor for a body strong
While other bodies flatten beds of pain.
No, not for these do I give thanks!

But I am grateful, Lord,
Because my meager loaf I may divide;
For that my busy hands
May move to meet another's need;
Because my doubled strength
I may expend to steady one who faints.
Yes, for all these do I give thanks!

For heart to share, desire to bear
And will to lift,
Flamed into one by deathless Love—
Thanks be to God for this!
Unspeakable! His Gift!

JANIE ALFORD

Better than Gold

Better than grandeur, better than gold,
Than rank and titles a thousandfold,
Is a healthy body and a mind at ease,
And simple pleasures that always please.
A heart that can feel for another's woe,
And share his joys with a genial glow;
With sympathies large enough to enfold
All men as brothers, is better than gold.

Better than gold is a conscience clear,
Though toiling for bread in an humble sphere,
Doubly blessed with content and health,
Untried by the lusts and cares of wealth,
Lowly living and lofty thought
Adorn and ennoble a poor man's cot;
For mind and morals in nature's plan
Are the genuine tests of an earnest man.

Better than gold is a peaceful home
Where all the fireside characters come,
The shrine of love, the heaven of life,
Hallowed by mother, or sister, or wife.
However humble the home may be,
Or tried with sorrow by heaven's decree,
The blessings that never were bought or sold,
And center there, are better than gold.

ABRAM J. RYAN

Life Owes Me Nothing

Life owes me nothing. Let the years
Bring clouds or azure, joy or tears;
    Already a full cup I've quaffed;
    Already wept and loved and laughed,
And seen, in ever-endless ways,
New beauties overwhelm the days.

Life owes me nought. No pain that waits
Can steal the wealth from memory's gates;
    No aftermath of anguish slow
    Can quench the soul fire's early glow.
I breathe, exulting, each new breath,
Embracing Life, ignoring Death.

Life owes me nothing. One clear morn
Is boon enough for being born;
    And be it ninety years or ten,
    No need for me to question when.
While Life is mine, I'll find it good,
And greet each hour with gratitude.

AUTHOR UNKNOWN

A Thankful Heart

Lord, Thou hast given me a cell
    Wherein to dwell,
A little house whose humble roof
    Is weatherproof . . .
Low is my porch as is my fate,
    Both void of state,
And yet the threshold of my door
    Is worn by the poor
Who hither come and freely get
    Good words or meat.
'Tis Thou that crown'st my glittering hearth
    With guiless mirth.
All these and better Thous dost send
    Me to this end,
That I should render for my part
    A thankful heart.

ROBERT HERRICK

Fulfillment

Lo, I have opened unto you the gates of my being,
And like a tide, you have flowed into me.
The innermost recesses of my spirit are full of you
And all the channels of my soul are grown sweet with
      your presence
For you have brought me peace;
    The peace of great tranquil waters,
And the quiet of the summer sea.
    Your hands are filled with peace as
The noon-tide is filled with light;
    About your head is bound the eternal
Quiet of the stars, and in your heart dwells the calm
      miracle of twilight.

I am utterly content.
In all my being is no ripple of unrest
    For I have opened unto you
The wide gates of my being
    And like a tide, you have flowed into me.

AUTHOR UNKNOWN

I Have Found Such Joy

I have found such joy in simple things;
    A plain, clean room, a nut-brown loaf of bread,
A cup of milk, a kettle as it sings,
    The shelter of a roof above my head,
And in a leaf-laced square along the floor,
Where yellow sunlight glimmers through a door.

I have found such joy in things that fill
    My quiet days: a curtain's blowing grace,
A potted plant upon my window sill,
    A rose, fresh-cut and placed within a vase;
A table cleared, a lamp beside a chair,
And books I long have loved beside me there.

Oh, I have found such joys I wish I might
    Tell every woman who goes seeking far
For some elusive, feverish delight,
    That very close to home the great joys are:
The elemental things—old as the race,
Yet never, through the ages, commonplace.

GRACE NOLL CROWELL

GRIEF

She Dwelt Among the Untrodden Ways

She dwelt among the untrodden ways
    Beside the springs of Dove,
A maid whom there were none to praise
    And very few to love:

A violet by a mossy stone
    Half hidden from the eye.
—Fair as a star, when only one
    Is shining in the sky.

She lived unknown, and few could know
    When Lucy ceased to be;
But she is in her grave, and, oh,
    The difference to me!

WILLIAM WORDSWORTH

We Kiss'd Again with Tears

As through the land at eve we went,
And pluck'd the ripen'd ears,
We fell out, my wife and I,
O we fell out I know not why,
And kiss'd again with tears.
And blessings on the falling out
That all the more endears,
When we fall out with those we love,
And kiss again with tears!
For when we came where lies the child
We lost in other years,
There above the little grave,
O there above the little grave,
We kiss'd again with tears.

ALFRED, LORD TENNYSON

O Captain! My Captain!

WRITTEN UPON HEARING OF THE ASSASSINATION
OF PRESIDENT ABRAHAM LINCOLN

O Captain! my Captain! our fearful trip is done,
The ship has weather'd every rack, the prize we
    sought is won,
The port is near, the bells I hear, the people all
    exulting,
While follow eyes the steady keel, the vessel grim and
    daring;
    But O heart! heart! heart!
      O the bleeding drops of red,
        Where on the deck my Captain lies,
        Fallen cold and dead.

O Captain! my Captain! rise up and hear the bells;
Rise up—for you the flag is flung—for you the bugle
    trills,
For you bouquets and ribbon'd wreaths—for you the
    shores a-crowding,
For you they call, the swaying mass, their eager faces
    turning;
    Here Captain! dear father!
      This arm beneath your head!
        It is some dream that on the deck,
        You've fallen cold and dead.

My Captain does not answer, his lips are pale and
      still,
My father does not feel my arm, he has no pulse nor
      will,
The ship is anchor'd safe and sound, its voyage closed
      and done,
From fearful trip the victor ship comes in with object
      won;
   Exult O shores, and ring O bells!
    But I with mournful tread,
       Walk the deck my Captain lies,
        Fallen cold and dead.

WALT WHITMAN

Miss You

I miss you in the morning, dear,
    When all the world is new;
I know the day can bring no joy
    Because it brings not you.
I miss the well-loved voice of you,
    Your tender smile for me,
The charm of you, the joy of your
    Unfailing sympathy.

The world is full of folks, it's true,
    But there was only one of you.

I miss you at the noontide, dear;
    The crowded city street
Seems but a desert now, I walk
    In solitude complete.
I miss your hand beside my own
    The light touch of your hand,
The quick gleam in the eyes of you
    So sure to understand.

The world is full of folks, it's true,
    But there was only one of you.

I miss you in the evening, dear,
    When daylight fades away;
I miss the sheltering arms of you
    To rest me from the day,
I try to think I see you yet
    There where the firelight gleams—
Weary at last, I sleep, and still
    I miss you in my dreams.

The world is full of folks, it's true,
    But there was only one of you.

AUTHOR UNKNOWN

No Place to Go

The happiest nights
    I ever know
Are those when I've
    No place to go,
And the missus says
    When the day is through:
"To-night we haven't
    A thing to do."

Oh, the joy of it,
    And the peace untold
Of sitting 'round
    In my slippers old,
With my pipe and book
    In my easy chair,
Knowing I needn't
    Go anywhere.

Needn't hurry
    My evening meal
Nor force the smiles
    That I do not feel,
But can grab a book
    From a near-by shelf,
And drop all sham
    And be myself.

Oh, the charm of it
    And the comfort rare;
Nothing on earth
    With it can compare;
And I'm sorry for him
    Who doesn't know
The joy of having
    No place to go.

EDGAR GUEST

Home

It takes a heap o' livin' in a house t' make it home,
A heap o' sun an' shadder, an' ye sometimes have t'
  roam
Afore ye really 'preciate the things ye lef' behind,
An' hunger fer 'em somehow, with 'em allus on yer
  mind.
It don't make any differunce how rich ye get t' be,
How much yer chairs an' tables cost, how great yer
  luxury;
It ain't home t' ye, though it be the palace of a king,
Until somehow yer soul is sort o' wrapped round
  everthing.

Home ain't a place that gold can buy or get up in a
  minute;
Afore it's home there's got t' be a heap o' livin' in it;
Within the walls there's got t' be some babies born,
  and then
Right there ye've got t' bring 'em up t' women good,
  an' men;
And gradjerly, as time goes on, ye find ye wouldn't
  part
With anything they ever used—they've grown into yer
  heart:

The old high chairs, the playthings, too, the little
      shoes they wore
Ye hoard; an' if ye could ye'd keep the thumb-marks
      on the door.

Ye've got t' weep t' make it home, ye've got t' sit an'
      sigh
An' watch beside a loved one's bed, an' know that
      Death is nigh;
An' in the stillness o' the night t' see Death's angel
      come,
An' close the eyes o' her that smiled, an' leave her
      sweet voice dumb.
Fer these are scenes that grip the heart, an' when yer
      tears are dried,
Ye find the home is dearer than it was, an' sanctified;
An' tuggin' at ye always are the pleasant memories
O' her that was an' is no more—ye can't escape from
      these.

Ye've got t' sing an' dance fer years, ye've got t' romp
      an' play,
An' learn t' love the things ye have by usin' 'em each
      day;

Even the roses 'round the porch must blossom year by
      year
Afore they 'come a part o' ye, suggestin' someone
      dear
Who used t' love 'em long ago, an' trained 'em jes' t'
      run
the way they do, so's they would get the early
      mornin' sun;
Ye've got t' love each brick an' stone from cellar up t'
      dome:
It takes a heap o' livin' in a house t' make it home.

EDGAR GUEST

Prayer for this House

May nothing evil cross this door,
And may ill fortune never pry
About these windows; may the roar
    And rain go by.

Strengthened by faith, these rafters will
Withstand the batt'ring of the storm;
This hearth, though all the world grow chill,
    Will keep us warm.

Peace shall walk softly through these rooms,
Touching our lips with holy wine,
Til ev'ry casual corner blooms
    Into a shrine.

Laughter shall drown the raucous shout;
And, though these shelt'ring walls are thin,
May they be strong to keep hate out
    And hold love in.

LOUIS UNTERMEYER

Home

Home!
My very heart's desire is safe
Within thy walls;
The voices of my loved ones, friends who come,
My treasured books that rest in niche serene,
All make more dear to me thy haven sweet.
Nor do my feet
Desire to wander out except that they
May have the glad return at eventide—
Dear Home.

Home!
My very heart's contentment lies
Within thy walls.
No worldly calls hath power to turn my eyes
In longing from thy quietness. Each morn
When I go forth upon the duties of the day
I wend my way
Content to know that eve will bring me
Safely to thy walls again.
Dear Home.

NELLIE WOMACK HINES

INSPIRATION

Beyond the Profit of Today

Lord, give me vision that shall see
    Beyond the profit of today
Into the years which are to be,
    That I may take the larger, wiser way.

I seek for fortune, Lord, nor claim
    To scorn the recompense I earn;
But help me, as I play the game,
    To give the world its just return.

Thou mad'st the earth for all of us,
    Teach me through struggle, strain and stress
To win and do my share, for thus
    Can profit lead to happiness.

Guard me from thoughts of little men
    Which blind the soul to greater things;
Save me from smug content and then
    From greed and selfishness it brings.

Aid me to join that splendid clan
    Of Business Men who seek to trace
A calm, considered working-plan
    To make the world a better place.

Teach me to hold this task above
    All lesser thoughts within my ken,
That thus I may be worthy of
    The name of Business Man; Amen!

AUTHOR UNKNOWN

The New Jerusalem

And did those feet in ancient time
    Walk upon England's mountains green?
And was the Holy Lamb of God
    On England's pleasant pastures seen?

And did the countenance divine
    Shine forth upon our clouded hills?
And was Jerusalem builded here
Among these dark satanic mills?

Bring me my bow of burning gold!
Bring me my arrows of desire!
Bring me my spear! O clouds, unfold!
    Bring me my chariot of fire!

I will not cease from mental fight,
    Nor shall my sword sleep in my hand,
Till we have built Jerusalem
    In England's green and pleasant land.

WILLIAM BLAKE

Be the Best of
Whatever You Are

If you can't be a pine on the top of the hill,
    Be a scrub in the valley—but be
The best little scrub by the side of the rill;
    Be a bush if you can't be a tree.

If you can't be a bust be a bit of the grass,
    And some highway happier make;
If you can't be a muskie than just be a bass—
    But the liveliest bass in the lake!

We can't all be captains, we've got to be crew,
    There's something for all of us here,
There's big work to do, and there's lesser to do,
    And the task you must do is the near.

If you can't be a highway than just be a trail,
    If you can't be the sun be a star;
It isn't by size that you win or you fail—
    Be the best of whatever you are!

DOUGLAS MALLOC

LOVE

Love

When love beckons to you, follow him,
Though his ways are hard and steep.
And when his wings enfold you yield to him.
Though the sword hidden among his pinions may
      wound you.
And when he speaks to you believe in him,
Though his voice may shatter your dreams as the
      north wind lays waste the garden.

For even as love crowns you so shall he crucify you.
    Even as he is for your growth so is he for your
    pruning.
Even as he ascends to your height and caresses your
    tenderest branches that quiver in the sun,
So shall he descend to your roots and shake them in
    their clinging to the earth.

Like sheaves of corn he gathers you unto himself.
He threshes you to make you naked.
He sifts you to free you from your husks.
He grinds you to whiteness.
He kneads you until you are pliant;
And then he assigns you to his sacred fire, that you
    may become sacred bread for God's sacred
    feast.

Love gives naught but itself and takes naught but
    from itself.
Love possesses not nor would it be possessed;
For love is sufficient unto love.

KAHLIL GIBRAN

Give All to Love

Give all to love;
Obey thy heart;
Friends, kindred, days,
Estate, good-fame,
Plans, credit, and the Muse—
Nothing refuse.

'Tis a brave master;
Let it have scope:
Follow it utterly,
Hope beyond hope:
High and more high
It dives into noon,
With wing unspent,
Untold intent;
But it is a god,
Knows its own path,
And the outlets of the sky.

It was not for the mean;
It requireth courage stout,
Souls above doubt,
Valor unbending;
Such 'twill reward—
They shall return
More than they were,
And ever ascending.

Leave all for love;
Yet, hear me, yet,
One word more thy heart behoved,
One pulse more of firm endeavor—
Keep thee today,
Tomorrow, forever,
Free as an Arab
Of thy beloved.

Cling with life to the maid;
But when the surprise,
First vague shadow of surmise
Flits across her bosom young
Of a joy apart from thee,
Free be she, fancy-free;
Nor thou detain her vesture's hem,
Nor the palest rose she flung
From her summer diadem.

Though thou loved her as thyself,
As a self of purer clay,
Though her parting dims the day,
Stealing grace from all alive;
Heartily know,
When half-gods go,
The gods arrive.

RALPH WALDO EMERSON

How Do I Love Thee?

How do I love thee? Let me count the ways.
   I love thee to the depth and breadth and height
   My soul can reach, when feeling out of sight
For the ends of Being and ideal Grace.
I love thee to the level of everyday's
   Most quiet need, by sun and candle-light.
   I love thee freely, as men strive for Right;
I love thee purely, as they turn from Praise.

   I love thee with the passion put to use
In my old griefs, and with my childhood's faith.
   I love thee with a love I seemed to lose
With my lost saints,—I love thee with the breath,
   Smiles, tears, of all my life!—and, if God choose,
I shall but love thee better after death.

ELIZABETH BARRETT BROWNING

Believe Me, If All Those Endearing Young Charms

Believe me, if all those endearing young charms,
 Which I gaze on so fondly today,
Were to change by tomorrow, and fleet in my arms,
 Like fairy-gifts fading away,
Thou wouldst still be adored, as this moment thou
  art,
 Let thy loveliness fade as it will,
And around the dear ruin each wish of my heart
 Would entwine itself verdantly still.

It is not while beauty and youth are thine own,
 And thy cheeks unprofaned by a tear,
That the fervour and faith of a soul can be known,
 To which time will but make thee more dear;
No, the heart that has truly loved never forgets,
 But as truly loves on to the close,
As the sunflower turns on her god, when he sets,
 The same look which she turned when he rose.

THOMAS MOORE

All Paths Lead to You

All paths lead to you
　　Where e'er I stray,
You are the evening star
　　At the end of day.

All paths lead to you
　　Hill-top or low,
You are the white birch
　　In the sun's glow.

All paths lead to you
　　Where e'er I roam.
You are the lark-song
　　Calling me home!

BLANCHE SHOEMAKER WAGSTAFF

Forgiven

You left me when the weary weight of sorrow
    Lay, like a stone, upon my bursting heart;
It seemed as if no shimmering tomorrow
    Could dry the tears that you had caused to start.
You left me, never telling why you wandered—
    Without a word, without a last caress;
Left me with but the love that I had squandered,
    The husks of love and a vast loneliness.

And yet if you came back with arms stretched toward me,
    Came back tonight, with carefree, smiling eyes,
And said: "My journeying has somehow bored me,
    And love, though broken, never, never dies!"
I would forget the wounded heart you gave me,
    I would forget the bruises on my soul.
My old-time gods would rise again to save me;
    My dreams would grow supremely new and whole.

What though youth lay, a tattered garment, o'er you?
    Warm words would leap upon my lips, long dumb;
If you came back, with arms stretched out before you,
    And told me, dear, that you were glad to come!

MARGARET E. SANGSTER

Miss You

Miss you, miss you, miss you;
    Everything I do
Echoes with the laughter
    And the voice of You.

You're on every corner,
    Every turn and twist,
Every old familiar spot
    Whispers how you're missed.

Miss you, miss you, miss you!
    Everywhere I go
There are poignant memories
    Dancing in a row.

Silhouette and shadow
    Of your form and face,
Substance and reality
    Everywhere displace.

Oh, I miss you, miss you!
   God! I miss you, Girl!
There's a strange, sad silence
   'Mid the busy whirl,

Just as tho' the ordinary
   Daily things I do
Wait with me, expectant
   For a word from You.

Miss you, miss you, miss you!
   Nothing now seems true
Only that 'twas heaven
   Just to be with You.

DAVID CORY

When We Two Parted

When we two parted
    In silence and tears,
Half broken-hearted
    To sever for years,
Pale grew thy cheek and cold,
    Colder thy kiss;
Truly that hour foretold
    Sorrow to this.

In secret we met—
    In silence I grieve
That thy heart could forget,
    Thy spirit deceive.
If I should meet thee
    After long years,
How should I greet thee?—
    With silence and tears.

GEORGE GORDON, LORD BYRON

A Bridge Instead of a Wall

They say a wife and husband, bit by bit,
  Can rear between their lives a mighty wall,
So thick they can not talk with ease through it,
  Nor can they see across, it stands so tall!
Its nearness frightens them but each alone
  Is powerless to tear its bulk away,
And each, dejected, wishes he had known
  For such a wall, some magic thing to say.

So let us build with master art, my dear,
  A bridge of faith between your life and mine,
A bridge of tenderness and very near
  A bridge of understanding, strong and fine—
    Till we have formed so many lovely ties
    There never will be room for walls to rise!

AUTHOR UNKNOWN

Marriage

You were born together, and together you shall be
      forevermore.
You shall be together when the white wings of death
      scatter your days.
Ay, you shall be together even in the silent memory
      of God.
But let there be spaces in your togetherness,
And let the winds of the heavens dance between you.

Love one another, but make not a bond of love:
Let it rather be a moving sea between the shores of
      your souls.
Fill each other's cup but drink not from one cup.
Give one another of your bread but eat not from the
      same loaf.
Sing and dance together and be joyous, but let each
      one of you be alone,
Even as the strings of a lute are alone though they
      quiver with the same music.

Give your hearts, but not into each other's keeping.
For only the hand of Life can contain your hearts.
And stand together yet not too near together:
For the pillars of the temple stand apart,
And the oak tree and the cypress grow not in each
other's shadow.

KAHLIL GIBRAN

Prayer of Any Husband

Lord, may there be no moment in her life
When she regrets that she became my wife,
And keep her dear eyes just a trifle blind
To my defects, and to my failings kind!

Help me to do the utmost that I can
To prove myself her measure of a man,
But, if I often fail as mortals may,
Grant that she never sees my feet of clay!

And let her make allowance—now and then—
That we are only grown-up boys, we men,
So, loving all our children, she will see,
Sometimes, a remnant of the child in me!

Since years must bring to all their load of care,
Let us together every burden bear,
And when Death beckons one its path along,
May not the two of us be parted long!

MAZIE V. CARUTHERS

Together

You and I by this lamp with these
Few books shut out the world. Our knees
Touch almost in this little space.
But I am glad. I see your face.
The silences are long, but each
Hears the other without speech.
And in this simple scene there is
The essence of all subtleties,
The freedom from all fret and smart,
The one sure sabbath of the heart.

The world—we cannot conquer it,
Nor change the minds of fools one whit.
Here, here alone do we create
Beauty and peace inviolate;
Here night by night and hour by hour
We build a high impregnable tower
Whence may shine, now and again,
A light to light the feet of men
When they see the rays thereof:
And this is marriage, this is love.

LUDWIG LEWISOHN

Husband and Wife

Whatever I said and whatever you said,
        I love you.
The word and the moment forever have fled;
        I love you.
The breezes may ruffle the stream in its flow,
But tranquil and clear are the waters below;
And under all tumult you feel and you know
        I love you.

Whatever you did and whatever I did,
        I love you.
Whatever is open, whatever is hid,
        I love you.
The strength of the oak makes the tempest a mock,
The anchor holds firm in the hurricane's shock;
Our love is the anchor, the oak and the rock.
        I love you.

Whatever I thought and whatever you thought,
        I love you.
The mood and the passion that made it are naught;
        I love you.
For words, thought and deeds, though they rankle
    and smart,
May never delude us or hold us apart
Who treasure this talisman deep in the heart,
        "I love you."

ARTHUR GUITERMAN

MEMORIES

Jenny Kiss'd Me

Jenny kiss'd me when we met,
　　Jumping from the chair she sat in;
Time, you thief, who love to get
　　Sweets into your list, put that in!
Say I'm weary, say I'm sad,
　　Say that health and wealth have miss'd me,
Say I'm growing old, but add,
　　Jenny kiss'd me.

LEIGH HUNT

Break, Break, Break

Break, break, break,
   On thy cold gray stones, O Sea!
And I would that my tongue could utter
   The thoughts that arise in me.

O well for the fisherman's boy,
   That he shouts with his sister at play!
O well for the sailor lad,
   That he sings in his boat on the bay!

And the stately ships go on
   To their haven under the hill;
But O for the touch of a vanished hand,
   And the sound of a voice that is still!

Break, break, break,
   At the foot of thy crags, O Sea!
But the tender grace of a day that is dead
   Will never come back to me.

ALFRED, LORD TENNYSON

What Lips My Lips Have Kissed, and Where, and Why

What lips my lips have kissed, and where, and why,
    I have forgotten, and what arms have lain
    Under my head till morning; but the rain
Is full of ghosts tonight, that tap and sigh
Upon the glass and listen for reply,
    And in my heart there stirs a quiet pain
    For unremembered lads that not again
Will turn to me at midnight with a cry.

Thus in the winter stands the lonely tree,
    Nor knows what birds have vanished one by one,
Yet knows its boughs more silent than before:
    I cannot say what loves have come and gone,
I only know that summer sang in me
A little while, that in me sings no more.

EDNA ST. VINCENT MILLAY

Tears, Idle Tears

Tears, idle tears, I know not what they mean,
Tears from the depth of some divine despair
Rise in the heart, and gather to the eyes,
In looking on the happy autumn-fields,
    And thinking of the days that are no more.

Fresh as the first beam glittering on a sail,
That brings our friends up from the underworld,
Sad as the last which reddens over one
That sinks with all we love below the verge;
    So sad, so fresh, the days that are no more.

Ah, sad and strange as in dark summer dawns
The earliest pipe of half-awakened birds
To dying ears, when unto dying eyes
The casement slowly grows a glimmering square;
    So sad, so strange, the days that are no more.

Dear as remembered kisses after death,
And sweet as those by hopeless fancy feigned
On lips that are for others; deep as love,
Deep as first love, and wild with all regret;
    O Death in Life, the days that are no more!

ALFRED, LORD TENNYSON

My Heart Leaps Up

My heart leaps up when I behold
    A rainbow in the sky:
So was it when my life began;
So is it now I am a man;
So be it when I shall grow old,
    Or let me die!
The Child is father of the Man;
And I could wish my days to be
Bound each to each by natural piety.

WILLIAM WORDSWORTH

Remembrance

This memory of my mother stays with me
    Throughout the years: the way she used to stand
    Framed in the door when any of her band
Of children left . . . as long as she could see
Their forms, she gazed, as if she seemed to be
    Trying to guard—to meet some far demand;
    And then before she turned to tasks at hand,
She breathed a little prayer inaudibly.

And now, I think, in some far heavenly place,
    She watches still, and yet is not distressed,
But rather as one who, after life's long race,
    Has found contentment in a well-earned rest,
There, in a peaceful, dreamlike reverie,
She waits, from earthly cares forever free.

MARGARET E. BRUNER

People Liked Him

People liked him, not because
    He was rich or known to fame;
He had never won applause
    As a star in any game.
His was not a brilliant style,
    His was not a forceful way,
But he had a gentle smile
    And a kindly word to say.

Never arrogant or proud,
    On he went with manner mild;
Never quarrelsome or loud,
    Just as simple as a child;
Honest, patient, brave and true:
    Thus he lived from day to day,
Doing what he found to do
    In a cheerful sort of way.

Wasn't one to boast of gold
    Or belittle it with sneers,
Didn't change from hot to cold,
    Kept his friends throughout the years,

Sort of man you like to meet
    Any time or any place.
There was always something sweet
    And refreshing in his face.

Sort of man you'd like to be:
    Balanced well and truly square;
Patient in adversity,
    Generous when his skies were fair.
Never lied to friend or foe,
    Never rash in word or deed,
Quick to come and slow to go
    In a neighbor's time of need.

. Never rose to wealth or fame,
    Simply lived, and simply died,
But the passing of his name
    Left a sorrow, far and wide.
Not for glory he'd attained,
    Nor for what he had of pelf,
Were the friends that he had gained,
    But for what he was himself.

EDGAR GUEST

MOTHER

Mother

As long ago we carried to your knees
    The tales and treasures of eventful days,
    Knowing no deed too humble for your praise,
Nor any gift too trivial to please,

So still we bring with older smiles and tears,
    What gifts we may to claim the old, dear right;
    Your faith beyond the silence and the night;
Your love still close and watching through the years.

AUTHOR UNKNOWN

Mother's Hands

Dear gentle hands have stroked my hair
    And cooled my brow,
Soft hands that pressed me close
    And seemed to know somehow
Those fleeting moods and erring thoughts
    That cloud my day,
Which quickly melt beneath their suffrage
    And pass away.

No other balm for earthly pain
    Is half so sure,
No sweet caress so filled with love
    Nor half so pure,
No other soul so close akin that understands,
No touch that brings such perfect peace as Mother's
       hands.

W. DAYTON WEDGEFARTH

The Old Mother

Poor old lady, set her aside—
    Her children are grown, and her work is done;
True, in their service, her locks turned gray,
    But shove her away, unsought, alone.

Give her a home, for decency's sake,
    In some back room, far out of the way,
Where her tremulous voice cannot be heard—
    It might check your mirth when you would be
        gay.

Strive to forget how she toiled for you
    And cradled you oft on her loving breast—
Told you stories and joined your play,
    Many an hour when she needed rest.

No matter for that—huddle her off;
    Your friends might wince at her unwitty jest;
She is too old-fashioned, and speaks so plain—
    Get her out of the way of the coming guest.

Once you valued her cheerful voice,
Her hearty laugh and her merry song;
But to ears polite they are quite too loud—
Her jokes too flat, her tales too long.

So, poor old lady, hustle her off—
In her cheerless room let her sit alone;
She must not meet with your guests tonight,
For her children are grown and her work is done.

AUTHOR UNKNOWN

Concord Hymn

By the rude bridge that arched the flood,
    Their flag to April's breeze unfurled,
Here once the embattled farmers stood,
    And fired the shot heard round the world.

The foe long since in silence slept;
    Alike the conqueror silent sleeps;
And Time the ruined bridge has swept
    Down the dark stream that seaward creeps.

Spirit, that made those heroes dare
    To die, and leave their children free,
Bid Time and Nature gently spare
    The shaft we raise to them and thee.

RALPH WALDO EMERSON

In Flanders Fields

In Flanders fields the poppies blow
Between the crosses, row on row,
    That mark our place; and in the sky
    The larks, still bravely singing, fly
Scarce heard amid the guns below.

We are the Dead. Short days ago
We lived, felt dawn, saw sunset glow,
    Loved and were loved, and now we lie
    In Flanders fields.

Take up our quarrel with the foe:
To you from failing hands we throw
    The torch; be yours to hold it high.
    If ye break faith with us who die
We shall not sleep, though poppies grow
    In Flanders fields.

JOHN McCRAE

The Soldier

If I should die, think only this of me;
    that there's some corner of a foreign field
That is forever England. There shall be
    In that rich earth a richer dust concealed;
A dust whom England bore, shaped, made aware,
    Gave, once, her flowers to love, her ways to
        roam,
A body of England's breathing English air,
    Washed by the rivers, blest by suns of home.

And think, this heart, all evil shed away,
    A pulse in the eternal mind, no less
        Gives somewhere back the thoughts by
          England given;
Her sights and sounds; dreams happy as her day;
    And laughter, learnt of friends; and gentleness,
        In hearts at peace, under an English heaven.

RUPERT BROOKE

Breathes There the Man with Soul So Dead

Breathes there the man, with soul so dead,
Who never to himself hath said,
 This is my own, my native land!
Whose heart hath ne'er within him burn'd
As home his footsteps he hath turn'd,
 From wandering on a foreign strand?
If such there breathe, go, mark him well;
For him no minstrel raptures swell;
High though his titles, proud his name,
Boundless his wealth as wish can claim,—
Despite those titles, power, and pelf,
The wretch, concentred all in self,
Living, shall forfeit fair renown,
And, doubly dying, shall go down
To the vile dust, from whence he sprung,
Unwept, unhonour'd, and unsung.

SIR WALTER SCOTT

PRAYER

For a New Home

Oh, love this house, and make of it a Home—
A cherished, hallowed place.
Root roses at its base, and freely paint
The glow of welcome on its smiling face!
For after friends are gone, and children marry,
And you are left alone . . .
The house you loved will clasp you to its heart,
Within its arms of lumber and of stone.

ROSA ZAGNONI MARINONI

A Prayer for Every Day

Make me too brave to lie or be unkind.
Make me too understanding, too, to mind
The little hurts companions give, and friends,
The careless hurts that no one quite intends.
Make me too thoughtful to hurt others so.
Help me to know
The inmost hearts of those for whom I care,
Their secret wishes, all the loads they bear,
That I may add my courage to their own.
May I make lonely folks feel less alone,
And happier ones a little happier yet.
May I forget
What ought to be forgotten; and recall,
Unfailing, all
That ought to be recalled, each kindly thing,
Forgetting what might sting.
To all upon my way,
Day after day,
Let me be joy, be hope! Let my life sing!

MARY CAROLYN DAVIES

Morning Prayer

When little things would irk me, and I grow
Impatient with my dear one, make me know
How in a moment joy can take its flight
And happiness be quenched in endless night.
Keep this thought with me all the livelong day
That I may guard the harsh words I might say
When I would fret and grumble, fiery hot,
At trifles that tomorrow are forgot—
Let me remember, Lord, how it would be
If these, my loved ones, were not here with me.

AUTHOR UNKNOWN

A Prayer Found in Chester Cathedral

Give me a good digestion, Lord
    And also something to digest;
Give me a healthy body, Lord,
    With sense to keep it at its best.

Give me a healthy mind, good Lord,
    To keep the good and pure in sight;
Which, seeing sin, is not appalled,
    But finds a way to set it right.

Give me a mind that is not bored,
    That does not whimper, whine or sigh;
Don't let me worry overmuch
    About the fussy thing called "I."

Give me a sense of humor, Lord,
    Give me the grace to see a joke;
To get some happiness from life,
    And pass it on to other folk.

AUTHOR UNKNOWN

A Morning Prayer

Let me today do something that will take
    A little sadness from the world's vast store,
And may I be so favored as to make
    Of joy's too scanty sum a little more.

Let me not hurt, by any selfish deed
    Or thoughtless word, the heart of foe or friend,
Nor would I pass unseeing worthy need,
    Or sin by silence when I should defend.

However meager by my worldly wealth,
    Let me give something that shall aid my kind—
A word of courage, or a thought of health
    Dropped as I pass for troubled hearts to find.

Let me tonight look back across the span
    Twixt dawn and dark, and to my conscience
      say—
Because of some good act to beast or man—
    "The world is better that I lived today."

ELLA WHEELER WILCOX

REFLECTIONS

Stanzas from the Rubaiyat of Omar Khayyam

Come, fill the Cup, and in the fire of Spring
Your Winter-garment of Repentance fling:
　　The Bird of Time has but a little way
To flutter—and the Bird is on the Wing.

Whether at Naishapur or Babylon,
Whether the Cup with sweet or bitter run,
　　The Wine of Life keeps oozing drop by drop,
The Leaves of Life keep falling one by one.

A Book of Verses underneath the Bough.
A Jug of Wine, a Loaf of Bread—and Thou
    Beside me singing in the Wilderness—
Ah, Wilderness were Paradise enow!

Some for the Glories of this World; and some
Sigh for the Prophet's Paradise to come;
    Ah, take the Cash, and let the Credit go,
Nor heed the rumble of a distant Drum!

When You and I behind the Veil are past,
Oh, but the long, long while the World shall last,
    Which of our Coming and Departure heeds
As the Sea's shore might heed a pebble cast.

The Moving Finger writes; and, having writ,
Moves on: nor all your Piety nor Wit
    Shall lure it back to cancel half a Line,
Nor all your Tears wash out a Word of it.

Ah Love! could but you and I conspire
To grasp this sorry Scheme of Things entire,
    Would we not shatter it to bits—and then
Remold it nearer to the Heart's Desire!

EDWARD FITZGERALD

On File

If an unkind word appears,
　　File the thing away.
If some novelty in jeers,
　　File the thing away.
If some clever little bit
Of a sharp and pointed wit,
Carrying a sting with it—
　　File the thing away.

If some bit of gossip come,
　　File the thing away.
Scandalously spicy crumb,
　　File the thing away.
If suspicion comes to you
That your neighbor isn't true
Let me tell you what to do—
　　File the thing away.

Do this for a little while,
Then go out and burn the file.

JOHN KENDRICK BANGS

The Garden of
Proserpine

Here, where the world is quiet;
 Here, where all trouble seems
Dead winds' and spent waves' riot
 In doubtful dreams of dreams;
I watch the green field growing
For reaping folk and sowing
For harvest-time and mowing,
 A sleepy world of streams.

I am tired of tears and laughter,
 And men that laugh and weep;
Of what may come hereafter
 For men that sow to reap:
I am weary of days and hours,
Blown buds of barren flowers,
Desires and dreams and powers
 And everything but sleep.

We are not sure of sorrow;
　　And joy was never sure;
Today will die tomorrow;
　　Time stoops to no man's lure;
And love, grown faint and fretful,
With lips but half regretful
Sighs, and with eyes forgetful
　　Weeps that no loves endure.

From too much love of living,
　　From hope and fear set free,
We thank with brief thanksgiving
　　Whatever gods may be
That no life lives for ever;
That dead men rise up never;
That even the weariest river
　　Winds somewhere safe to sea.

ALGERNON SWINBURNE

Dover Beach

The sea is calm to-night.
The tide is full, the moon lies fair
Upon the straits;—on the French coast the light
Gleams and is gone; the cliffs of England stand
Glimmering and vast, out in the tranquil bay.

Come to the window, sweet is the night-air!
Only, from the long line of spray
Where the sea meets the moon-blanch'd land,
Listen! you hear the grating roar
Of pebbles which the waves draw back, and fling,
At their return, up the high strand,
Begin, and cease, and then again begin,
With tremulous cadence slow, and bring
The eternal note of sadness in.

Sophocles long ago
Heard it on the Aegean, and it brought
Into his mind the turbid ebb and flow,
Of human misery; we
Find also in the sound a thought,
Hearing it by this distant northern sea.

The Sea of Faith
Was once, too, at the full, and round earth's shore
Lay like the folds of a bright girdle furl'd.
But now I only hear
Its melancholy, long, withdrawing roar,
Retreating, to the breath
Of the night-wind, down the vast edges drear
And naked shingles of the world.

Ah, love, let us be true
To one another! for the world, which seems
To lie before us like a land of dreams,
So various, so beautiful, so new,
Hath really neither joy, nor love, nor light,
Nor certitude, nor peace, nor help for pain;
And we are here as on a darkling plain
Swept with confused alarms of struggle and flight,
Where ignorant armies clash by night.

MATTHEW ARNOLD

THOUGHTFULNESS

Those We Love the Best

One great truth in life I've found,
　　While journeying to the West—
The only folks we really wound
　　Are those we love the best.

The man you thoroughly despise
　　Can rouse your wrath, 'tis true;
Annoyance in your heart will rise
　　At things mere strangers do.

But those are only passing ills;
   This rule all lives will prove;
The rankling wound which aches and thrills
   Is dealt by hands we love.

The choicest garb, the sweetest grace,
   Are oft to strangers shown;
The careless mien, the frowning face,
   Are given to our own.

We flatter those we scarcely know,
   We please the fleeting guest,
And deal full many a thoughtless blow
   To those we love the best. . . .

ELLA WHEELER WILCOX

The Sin of Omission

It isn't the thing you do;
    It's the thing you leave undone,
Which gives you a bit of heartache
    At the setting of the sun.

The tender word forgotten,
    The letter you did not write,
The flower you might have sent,
    Are your haunting ghosts tonight.

The stone you might have lifted
    Out of a brother's way,
The bit of heartsome counsel
    You were hurried too much to say.

The loving touch of the hand,
    The gentle and winsome tone,
That you had no time or thought for
    With troubles enough of your own.

The little acts of kindness,
    So easily out of mind;
Those chances to be helpful
    Which everyone may find—

No, it's not the thing you do,
    It's the thing you leave undone,
Which gives you the bit of heartache
    At the setting of the sun.

MARGARET E. SANGSTER

Our Own

If I had known in the morning
  How wearily all the day
The words unkind would trouble my mind
  That I said when you went away,
I had been more careful, darling,
  Nor given you needless pain;
But we vex our own with look and tone
  We may never take back again.

For though in the quiet evening
  You may give me the kiss of peace,
Yet it well might be that never for me
  The pain of the heart should cease!
How many go forth at morning
  Who never come home at night!
And hearts have broken for harsh words spoken
  That sorrow can ne'er set right.

We have careful thought for the stranger,
    And smiles for the sometime guest;
But oft for "our own" the bitter tone,
    Though we love our own the best.
Ah! lips with the curve impatient,
    Ah! brow with the shade of scorn,
'Twere a cruel fate, were the night too late
    To undo the work of the morn!

MARGARET E. SANGSTER

If I Had Known

If I has known what trouble you were bearing;
What griefs were in the silence of your face;
I would have been more gentle, and more caring,
And tried to give you gladness for a space.
I would have brought more warmth into the place,
　　If I had known.

If I had known what thoughts despairing drew you;
(Why do we never try to understand?)
I would have lent a little friendship to you,
And slipped my hand within your hand,
And made you stay more pleasant in the land,
　　If I had known.

MARY CAROLYN DAVIES

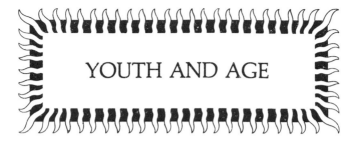

YOUTH AND AGE

How Old Are You?

Age is a quality of mind.
If you have left your dreams behind,
    If hope is cold,
If you no longer look ahead,
If your ambitions' fires are dead—
    Then you are old.

But if from life you take the best,
And if in life you keep the jest,
    If love you hold;
No matter how the years go by,
No matter how the birthdays fly—
    You are not old.

H.S. FRITSCH

To Youth

This I say to you:
Be arrogant! Be true!
True to April's lust that sings
Through your veins. These sharp Springs
Matter most . . . After years
Will be time enough to sleep . . .
Carefulness . . . and tears . . .

Now while life is raw and new,
Drink it clear, drink it deep!
Let the moonlight's lunacy
Tear away your cautions.
Be proud, and mad, and young, and free!
Grasp a comet! Kick at stars
Laughingly! Fight! Dare!
Arms are soft, breasts are white.
Magic's in the April night—

Never fear, Age will catch you,
Slow you down, ere it dispatch you
To your long and solemn quiet . . .
What will matter then the riot
Of the lilacs in the wind?
What will mean—then—the crush
Of lips at hours when birds hush?
Purple, green and flame will end
In a calm, gray blend.

Only graven in your soul
After all the rest is gone
There will be ecstacies . . .
These alone . . .

JOHN WEAVER

When I Was One-and-Twenty

When I was one-and-twenty
   I heard a wise man say,
"Give crowns and pounds and guineas
   But not your heart away;
Give pearls away and rubies
   But keep your fancy free."
But I was one-and-twenty,
   No use to talk to me.

When I was one-and-twenty
   I heard him say again,
"The heart out of the bosom
   Was never given in vain;
'Tis paid with sighs a-plenty
   And sold for endless rue."
And I am two-and-twenty,
   And oh, 'tis true, 'tis true.

A.E. HOUSMAN

Growing Old

The days grow shorter, the nights grow longer;
　　The headstones thicken along the way;
And life grows sadder, but love grows stronger
　　For those who walk with us day by day.

The tear comes quicker, the laugh comes slower;
　　The courage is lesser to do and dare;
And the tide of joy in the heart falls lower,
　　And seldom covers the reefs of care.

But all true things in the world seem truer,
　　And the better things of earth seem best,
And friends are dearer, as friends are fewer,
　　And love is all as our sun dips west.

Then let us clasp hands as we walk together,
　　And let us speak softly in low, sweet tone,
For no man knows on the morrow whether
　　We two pass on—or but one alone.

ELLA WHEELER WILCOX

INDEX OF FIRST LINES

INDEX OF AUTHORS

ACKNOWLEDGMENTS

Thanks to the following publishers for their permission to reprint the poems listed:

ON CHILDREN, ON FRIENDSHIP, ON LOVE, ON MARRIAGE reprinted from *The Prophet*, by Kahlil Gibran, with permission of the publisher, Alfred A. Knopf, Inc. Copyright 1923 by Kahlil Gibran; renewal copyrite 1951 by Administrators C.T.A. of Kahlil Gibran Estate, and Mary G. Gibran.

ONLY A DAD, FATHER, ON GOING HOME FOR CHRISTMAS, NO PLACE TO GO, HOME, THE JUNK BOX, PEOPLE LIKED HIM, DEFEAT from *The Collected Poems of Edgar Guest*, with permission of Contemporary Books, Inc.

PRAYER FOR THIS HOUSE from *This Singing World* edited by Louis Untermeyer, copywright 1923 by Hartcourt Brace Jovanovich, Inc; renewed 1951 by Louis Untermeyer. Reprinted by permission of the publisher.

REMEMBRANCE by Margaret E. Bruner, Indianapolis Sunday Star.

THE SOLDIER by Rupert Brooke, reprinted by permission of Dodd, Mead & Company, Inc., from *The Collected Poems of Rupert Brooke*. Copyright 1915 by Dodd, Mead & Company. Copyright renewed 1943 by Edward March. Thanks to McClelland & Stewart of Toronto, Ontario, Canada, for permission to reprint this poem in Canada.

TREES by Joyce Kilmer. Copyright 1913 and renewed 1941. Copyright assigned to Jerry Vogel Music Co., Inc., 58 West 45th Street, New York, N.Y. 10036. Used by permission of copyright owner. Reproduction prohibited.

WECOME OVER THE DOOR OF AN OLD INN, HUSBAND AND WIFE by Arthur Guiterman, with permission of Louise H. Sclove.

WHAT LIPS MY LIPS HAVE KISSED from *Collected Poems*, Harper & Row. Copyright 1923, 1928, 1951, 1955 Edna St. Vincent Millay and Norma Millay Ellis.

WHAT THOMAS AN BUILE SAID IN A PUB reprinted with permission of Macmillan Publishing Co., Inc., from COLLECTED POEMS by James Stephens. Thanks to Mrs. Iris Wise and Macmillan, London and Basingstoke for permission to reprint this poem in the British Commonwealth.

WHEN I WAS ONE—AND—TWENTY by A.E. Housman from *A Shropshire Lad*—Authorized Edition—from *The Collected Poems of A.E. Housman*. Copyright 1939, 1940, © 1965 by Holt, Rinehart and Winston. Copyright © 1967, 1968 by Robert E. Symons. Reprinted by permission of Holt, Rinehart and Winston, Publishers. Thanks to the Society of Authors, London, England, for permission to reprint this poem in Canada and the United Kingdom.

Thanks to the following authors for permission to reprint the poems listed:

Janie Alford, THANKS BE TO GOD

Bertha Adams Backus, THEN LAUGH

John Kendrick Bangs, ON FILE

Anne Campbell, TO MY FRIEND,
    THERE IS ALWAYS A PLACE FOR YOU

Mazie V. Caruthers, PRAYER OF ANY HUSBAND

David Cory, MISS YOU

Roy Croft, LOVE

Grace Noll Crowell, I HAVE FOUND SUCH JOY

Mary Carolyn Davies, A PRAYER FOR EVERY DAY,
IF I HAD KNOWN

H.N. Fifer, WHAT WAS HIS CREED?

Sam Walter Foss, THE HOUSE BY THE SIDE OF THE ROAD

Spencer Michael Free, THE HUMAN TOUCH

H.S. Fritsch, HOW OLD ARE YOU?

Ethel Romig Fuller, TODAY

Wilfred Wilson Gibson, THE STONE

Margaret Johnston Griffin, TO MY SON

Nellie Womach Hines, HOME

Nick Kenny, PATTY-POEM

Ludwig Lewisohn, TOGETHER

Douglas Malloch, BE THE BEST OF WHATEVER YOU ARE

Rosa Zagnoni Marinoni, FOR A NEW HOME

John McCrae, IN FLANDERS FIELDS

Louis I. Newman, THE VOICE OF GOD

Joseph Parry, NEW FRIENDS AND OLD FRIENDS

Mary Davis Reed, ONE YEAR TO LIVE

Abram J. Ryan, BETTER THAN GOLD

Margaret E. Sanster, A PRAYER FOR FAITH, FORGIVEN, THE SIN OF OMISSION, OUR OWN

R.L. Sharpe, A BAG OF TOOLS

Charles Swain, TAKE THE WORLD AS IT IS

Charles Hanson Towne, AT NIGHTFALL

Blanche Shoemaker Wagstaff, ALL PATHS LEAD TO YOU

John Weaver, TO YOUTH

W. Dayton Wedgefarth, MOTHER'S HANDS

Ruth Winant Wheeler, PRAYER FOR SHUT-INS

Diligent effort has been made to credit all the authors of the poems in this volume. Yet in some cases we have not succeeded in tracking down the address of the copyright owner or of the copyright owner's successor in interest. Where we have been unable to accord proper credit, forgiveness is implored.

A HART BOOK

A & W PUBLISHERS
New York